THE
TOP-DOLLAR
MINDSET

12 Secrets for Selling Your House

THE
TOP-DOLLAR
MINDSET

12 Secrets for Selling Your House

JAMIE LEE MOORE

THE TOP-DOLLAR MINDSET:

12 Secrets for Selling Your House.

ISBN: 978-0-578-01527-9

Printed in the United States of America.

For information, contact Jamie Lee Moore, 700 Larkspur Landing Circle, Suite 199, Larkspur, CA 94939, www.jlmrealestate.com.

• *Contents* •

• *Secret One* •
THE TOP-DOLLAR MINDSET

• *Secret Two* •
THE HIDDEN CRITERIA OF HOME BUYERS

• *Secret Three* •
CLEAN IT, STAGE IT & GET OUT

• *Secret Four* •
ELIMINATE OR MINIMIZE BUYER TURN-OFFS

• *Secret Ten* •
MAKE MONEY BY NEGOTIATING

• *Secret Eleven* •
HIRE AN AGENT WHO WILL MAKE YOU MONEY

• *Secret Twelve* •
FOR SALE BY OWNER:
SAVE THE COMMISSION, LOSE TOP-DOLLAR

ACKNOWLEDGEMENTS

I thank the following friends and family for their insights, support, information and encouragement for the creation of this book: Trudy Brands, William Brands, Danielle Brands, Alice Tanner, Jack Heffron, Mark K. Sorensen of California Pacific Mortgage, Joy Gray of Joy Gray Design, Carlis Collins, Kenneth Baker, Ira Smith, Carol Moore, Ozzy Gershon, Trey McAlister and Jean O'Neill of Productive Learning and Leisure, LLC.

I give special thanks to Thomas Moore and Margie Miller for helping me think this book into being.

INTRODUCTION

All home sellers think their home is worth more than agents and home buyers and they usually receive less money than they expect when they sell their home.

Why is this so?

Most often it is because they want top-dollar for their house, but they do not realize they must have a *top-dollar mindset* to earn top-dollar.

To have a *top-dollar mindset* means you understand that everything you do - or do not do - affects the price you earn from the sale of your home.

The secrets of a *top-dollar mindset* contained in these pages go beyond the laundry lists and tips and tricks found in other books. Examples are used throughout this book illustrating how to capitalize on a top-dollar decision making mindset when you sell your home, regardless of market conditions.

If you are having trouble selling your home, are thinking about selling your home in the immediate future, or are about to list your home for sale, you must utilize the top-dollar mindset to maximize your home selling profits.

THE
TOP-DOLLAR
MINDSET

12 Secrets for Selling Your House

· *Secret One* ·

THE TOP-DOLLAR MINDSET

Whether selling your home in a buyer's market, or seller's market, you can achieve maximum profits for your home by acting with a top-dollar mindset.

The top-dollar mindset is a simple attitude and understanding that every single choice you make about preparing your home for sale, hiring an agent, showing it to prospective buyers and negotiating the sale, will either earn you money or cost you money.

To get top-dollar, you must practice the top-dollar mindset, and become aware of the actions and decisions you make concerning the sale of your home.

CHOICES CAN MAKE YOU MONEY

Stop yourself and ask if the action or choice you are about to take is likely to:

- *make you money;*
- *save you money; or*
- *become a money drain or leave money on the table.*

Of course, it is not realistic to do everything imaginable to get the maximum price ever possible due to your money and time constraints. However, you can maximize the dollars earned from the sale of your home by using the top-dollar mindset when possible.

Think of it this way: To get top-dollar, you must close the gap between the as-is price and the top-dollar price.

This maximum price you earn, taking into account your time, energy and money constraints, *is top-dollar* for your particular home in your market when you sell it. It is the highest price you can earn given your situation and the conscious choices you make.

UNCONSCIOUS CHOICES COST YOU MONEY

You will lose money if you make unconscious choices based on what is convenient or easy for you. If you make expensive unconscious choices they will leave you wondering why you did not earn as much as you expected for your house.

If you fail to sell your home for top-dollar, it is because your choices and actions have eroded the dollars your home could earn. In your mind, you may think that you need to do nothing to earn top-dollar. In reality, every home seller must do some inconvenient things, and make efforts, to earn the top-dollar price they have in their minds for the sale of their house.

HOW TO USE THE TOP-DOLLAR MINDSET

One way to use the top-dollar mindset is demonstrated by a simple example involving clutter.

Everyone hates clutter, but everyone loves their collections and their stuff (a.k.a clutter). Assume a home seller has an enormous award-winning doll collection that has literally taken over the house to the point where there is a doll everywhere you look.

The home seller who is lacking the top-dollar mindset may decide to leave the collection on display because it is too much work to pack it all away; there is not enough time to pack it all away; it is not good for the dolls to be packed away; or because they are just so proud of the award winning collection, they do not *want* to pack the dolls away. Sometimes these home sellers *say* they will pack them away, only to leave the collection out when the day comes to list or show the house. This disastrous decision to leave the collection on display may be conscious or unconscious.

Since they do not have a top-dollar mindset, it never occurs to the doll loving home sellers that they will earn money, in the form of a higher offer, for each doll they pack and cart away from the buyer's view; but it is true!

Home buyers offer more money and are more eager to buy a spacious home. Clutter free homes feel spacious. Buyers and agents walk away from a cluttered house with a bad impression because they are distracted by the collection of clutter and cannot *see the forest for the trees*. In a month or so, the seller, impatient for an offer, will not recognize that their own decision to leave the collection in full view is to blame. When an offer finally arrives, they will wonder why it is so low. They sell their house without the clear understanding that they could have earned more money had they removed the doll collection.

In the case of clutter, sellers who use the top-dollar mindset must envision carrying a box of dollar bills to their bank each time they carry a box of their stuff to storage, because, in essence, this is the truth.

Like the doll collector, there are things you will not do to close the gap between the as-is price for your home and the top-dollar price. That is all right. If you leave money on the table because it is not worth the effort; so be it. Your objective is to capture as many dollars as possible within your time, money, and energy limitations. You do not have to capture every dollar, just be aware that certain choices you make will either make you money or cost you money.

You will have the *top-dollar mindset* when you understand and are conscious that every choice you make when selling your home is one that will earn you money, save you money, or drain your money away.

• Secret Two •
THE HIDDEN CRITERIA OF HOME BUYERS

If you want top-dollar for your house, you must make choices that give home buyers what they want. But what, exactly, do they want? Granite counter tops, remodeled kitchens and baths, huge master suites, high ceilings, a wide open feeling and a great view, right?

That is all true but what if you cannot afford to remodel? Are you destined to fail and get the as-is price for your home? Should you even bother to prepare your house for showings? What can you do to maximize your gains if your home offers none of these bells and whistles?

BUYERS MUST FEEL INSPIRED

Home is the most important place in the world to each and every person on earth. Whether it is a small one bedroom condo walking distance to work, or a sprawling one-thousand acre ranch in the middle of nowhere, home is the most important place in the world because it gives people the life they want to live. People are always searching for a better life, and sometimes that includes a new home that offers them a better life according to their own personal dream.

The standard criteria of home buyers include the number of bedrooms, baths, fireplaces, pools, garages, parking spaces and the like. The *secret criterion* of home buyers is they are not just searching for a new home with these attributes; they are searching for a new and better life. This is the primary secret you must understand to successfully sell your house for top-dollar in any market. You must use this secret as your guiding light when preparing your home for the market.

If home buyers feel inspired by the life they imagine living in your home, they cannot wait to buy your home. They will offer more for it because inspiration is an intangible feeling that adds tremendous value to everything it touches. Home buyers will literally pay you extra for these feelings about living in your home.

So, how exactly can you use this secret as a guiding light? What does it mean?

The Universal Recipe for Inspiration

Home buyers all want the same thing: open floor plan, plenty of light, and a wide open feeling with views of nature through their windows. This is a universal recipe for inspiration. Strive to provide a feeling of spaciousness, light and openness. You can do this even in small places. These feelings are universally inspiring, so make it so to inspire and maximize your returns.

Ask Yourself: What Inspired Me?

If you have the top-dollar mindset, you will ask yourself what inspired you to buy the house. The chances are good that what inspired you to buy the house will also inspire a buyer to buy the house from you. If it was the views, enhance their impact. If it was the kitchen, make the kitchen glisten and ready to throw the house warming party a home buyer easily visualizes. If the yard beckoned you; make it beckon them.

Emphasize the lifestyle, not just the attributes of the home, in your marketing materials and your presentation of the home.

INSPIRATION LEADS TO MOTIVATION

Home buyers must walk into the house and see and feel a clean, easy, stress-free, beautiful, comfortable and convenient life in the house before they consider leaving their existing home to buy your house. This means you must present your house in a way that not only *inspires*, but also *motivates* them to leave their existing life and buy the life your house offers them.

They express inspired feelings by saying things like the house *feels like my house* or *it just feels right* or *feels comfortable. Wow* is a common one. When you hear these phrases, they mean the buyer *feels inspired.* That inspired feeling is the juice that motivates them to trade the life they are now living for the life they hope, feel and believe they will be living in the house if they buy it from you. This is your goal. You want buyers to walk into your house and say these things – however you manage it.

Of course, you need not completely rebuild or remodel your home. Work with what you have and make it sing according to your budget and time.

Inspiration Comes from a *Feeling* in Your Home

What if you already spent a lot of money on upgrades like a new foundation, new windows and earthquake retrofitting? Home buyers never say they are *inspired* by the new foundation earthquake retrofitting or by the new windows.

Inspiration comes from the *feeling* buyers have in your home.

Foundation and earthquake upgrades are important but do not give buyers immediate *feelings* about a home. These types of upgrades cause additional good feelings through their rational thinking, but they do not trump the feeling of inspiration necessary to motivate them to appreciate the upgrades.

Making foundation repairs and installing new energy efficient windows are important and you should do these things; after all, they are part of the package that justifies your list price. But make no mistake; buyers must first buy your house with their heart, before these efforts will pay off. Your rule of thumb is: Heart first. Head second.

When Inspiration is Lacking

If you fail to inspire, or provide only lack luster feelings of inspiration, the value of your home goes down in the hearts of buyers and you earn less for it than you might earn if you provide powerful and positive feelings of inspiration in the home.

If you do not believe this, why do you think home buyers decide against purchasing a particular house even if it meets all of the attributes on their list? Because this is not their *true criteria*! A home buyer's true criteria are only partly comprised of the number of bedrooms, baths, etc. These are a given. The most powerful, but hidden, criterion of home buyers is the house must offer the perception of *a better life than the one I live now.* This inspiration is what motivates them to investigate the details, write an offer and move in.

When a home lacks inspiration, buyers say it is *missing something, doesn't have that wow factor* or *it just doesn't feel quite right.* Put simply: They don't write an offer.

When inspiration is lacking, home sellers wait longer for an offer and receive less money for their house. This is because the inspiration they are giving is not enough to motivate. Some home sellers will take only minimal actions to make a home acceptable. This is a mistake because they are leaving a lot of money on the table for the buyer instead of putting it into their own bank account. Others clean, stage and do all kinds of things to make the house appealing but fail to provide adequate inspiration to motivate buyers. If this is your situation, ramp up the inspiration as quickly as possible.

Authentic Inspiration

This leads to another key point regarding inspiration: Behind each home buyer are real estate agents, friends, family, advisors and naysayers. You must not only inspire the buyers, but remember these other people must also feel inspired or they can put a damper on the buyer's enthusiasm. This means your house must offer authentic inspiration; not mere window dressing, before a buyer will offer top-dollar for your house.

THE DREAM PREMIUM

If your house inspires a lot of home buyers and the price makes sense to them, you earn a *dream premium*. This occurs when your house is priced at market value, meets the inspiration, dream and price requirements of more than one home buyer in any given market and you receive multiple offers. Multiple offers mean you earn your particular top-dollar plus a little bit more. That little bit more is the *dream premium* which equates to *hopes* and *dreams* or *universal inspiration*. This happens *even in a buyer's market*. This is your reward for providing true inspiration to more than one home buyer.

Fool's Gold

Selling your home *quick* does not necessarily mean you earned the dream premium.

If you are selling in a strong seller's market, you may receive multiple offers because the demand for homes outstrips the supply of homes available for sale. If you price your home far below market value, regardless of market conditions, you may receive multiple offers because the price was too good to be true. Multiple offers in these scenarios do not necessarily mean you are earning the dream premium. You might be earning mere as-is value.

Use your top-dollar mindset to provide inspiration and motivation to get the dream premium AND sell your home quick if that is your desire.

• *Secret Three* •
CLEAN IT, STAGE IT & GET OUT

Home buyers pay more for beautiful homes that make them feel alive and inspired. They pay more for clean homes. They pay more for homes that look easy to live in and that are spacious and bright. They pay more for homes that require little or no work, i.e., homes which are *turn-key* or *move-in-ready*.

If you have the *top-dollar mindset*, you will make your home appeal to those buyers who will want to pay more for those feelings and conveniences. If you do not have the top-dollar mindset, and do not make your home look and feel clean and easy, you are leaving money on the table.

So, what exactly must you do?

CLEAN IT

You must present a clean and organized house before you open it to prospective buyers and agents. This means everything you see, and everything you cannot see, must be clean and organized.

Clean the Unseen

It is a mistake to de-clutter the main areas of the house by stuffing your possessions into storage sheds, closets and drawers.

News Flash!

Home buyers look inside closets, drawers and storage areas to see if they can fit their stuff into those spaces and still have room for the other things they plan for their new life, such as big screen TVs, kayaks, bikes, pets, babies and mothers-in-law.

If your closets and cupboards are grimy, dusty, need paint, stuffed full, disorganized, or if items fall out when the door is opened, buyers will not pay top-dollar, let alone, the dream premium, for your house. More likely, you will have to pay them to take your cluttered closet!

Do Not Allow Money to Slip Through Your Fingers

If you cannot grasp this concept then this is the bottom line: You are allowing money to slip through your fingers when you sell a dirty or cluttered house. Bank owned houses and foreclosed homes sell for less, in part, because they are not clean and easy. They convey exhaustion.

It is often feelings of disorganization, a need for more space, or the dream of having a clean house, that *cause* home buyers to seek a new house. Give this to them. Fill their emotional need for these things. If you do, they will reward you with more money for your house. Remember: it's not just a house they are seeking, but a new life. If you do not give them what they want and need, they will move on to another house whose sellers understand their hidden criteria and give it to them.

Toss Expired Foods & Medicines

Throw away all expired foods, medicines and cleaning products. All other medicines and prescriptions must be placed in private drawers. Stagers sum it up as follows: *Nobody is sick in this house.* Psychologically, no one wants to buy a house if there are sick people living in it, right? As you remove these items, just remember that for each item you remove, you are adding dollars to your sale price.

Feed the Plants

The same goes for plants, landscaping and messy yards – *especially messy front yards*. Your plants must look alive, nourished and vibrant. Dead plants, dying plants, dried flowers or artificial flowers must go. They make houses dirty, stagnate and lifeless. Home buyers want to feel that your house will nourish them, make them grow and feel alive. Removing these items is taking money to the bank.

Finish Repairs Before You List

Repairs are messy. Make all repairs and paint touch ups *before* you list and show your house. Too many sellers put the finishing touches on paint, small repairs, or even large repairs, during or after the first few showings. This is a huge mistake. The repairs must be complete before the house is shown to prospective buyers and agents. When buyers and agents walk into a house, you do not want them thinking about the messy half-finished repair job, the door knob that needs replacing, the wall that still needs paint or the landscaping that needs planting. These thoughts are distracting and reduce your sale price.

You are probably thinking it is no big deal if you still have *some* of these repairs in progress during the initial thirty days your house is on the market. That is not a *top-dollar mindset*. Those little fix-it items do not go unnoticed and the buyers, consciously or unconsciously, reduce their offer for each little repair and repair mess they see. They always take off more money in their minds than it actually costs to make those repairs. Fix the items so they never enter the buyer's mind and remember: you are taking money to your bank for each item you fix.

The President is Coming!

Imagine that the President of the United States is coming to visit. If your house is clean enough for the president and the news crew, then you are finished!

Make sure all cobwebs and lint are vacuumed from window coverings and ceilings. Clear all dust from mini blinds, lamps, light fixtures, base boards and door casings. Clean all appliances. All windows must be spotless. It is best to take down window screens and keep all window coverings open. Replace all bathroom caulk. Clean under beds and furniture.

Make the house spotless before it hits the market. Once you have the house thoroughly cleaned, clean it once a week to keep the dust and smells to a minimum.

STAGE IT

This brings me to a common mistake: lack of staging. A seller whose home is not staged is leaving thousands of dollars on the table. Not hundreds; but thousands.

It's A Pottery Barn® World.

Staging a house is no longer an option. We live in a Pottery Barn® world. Buyers expect staged houses and find it difficult to become inspired by a house that is not staged.

Think about it. Why do you think new home builders spend

thousands of dollars decorating model homes? It's because they have the top-dollar mindset. They know they must provide a dream, an inspired feeling, to earn top-dollar for the houses they build and sell.

Staging Is a Matter of Degree

The amount, and type, of staging you need to achieve top-dollar is a matter of degree. At one end of the spectrum is full staging of all rooms with all new furnishings. At the other end of the spectrum is staging with the items you have but presenting them in a more emotionally appealing arrangement.

For example, if you have beautiful furniture and furnishings, you may only need a stager to move the furniture and add and subtract items to enhance inspiration. If your furnishings are sparse, you may need plants, lamps, rugs and accessories to pull it all together to enhance the warmth of the home. If you have an empty home with a perplexing floor plan, you must stage to demonstrate how to use the spaces.

Staging need not be expensive or difficult. There are some rules to follow to maximize the positive impact staging can have on your sale price.

Stage Before You List

The first rule of staging is you must stage the house *before* you take the advertising photos and always, always, stage your house *before* you list it for sale.

Occasionally, sellers who know that staging will get them top-dollar nevertheless take a chance and try to sell their house for top-dollar without staging. When the house fails to sell a month later, they decide staging is probably a good idea.

Sellers who stage after the house is put on the market only waste their money on staging and are better off taking the house off the market for thirty to sixty days so they can stage it and bring it back on the market as a fresh new listing. Staging in the middle of a listing period costs you time and money – especially if you are making payments for a vacant house.

In rare circumstances, agents fail to include photos of the house in their advertising. This sends a message to buyers that the house is ugly, uninspiring and not worth seeing. You do not want your house advertising to give this impression. If this is true, just wave goodbye to thousands of dollars.

Hire a Talented Stager

The second rule of staging is hire a professional stager or organizer. If you want top-dollar, do not let your real estate agent stage the house and do not do it yourself – even if you have a degree in interior decorating. Why? Stagers come into your house looking at it from a buyer's perspective, not from the perspective of liking the lamps you bought in Morocco or the way your couch faces the television. They put on their *buyer glasses* and give buyers what they want. They enhance the qualities of your house without distracting with furniture. They are not present during the open houses to boast about their decorating acumen. The best stagers understand what to do if you ask them to *inspire* home buyers.

Make sure the staging costs are reasonable and the stager is talented. Obtain bids from two or more stagers/organizers and compare their bids: apples to apples. Look at other houses they have staged. Ask them how long the houses were on the market and how much the sellers received for the house as compared to their list price. Call their references and ask agents who have worked with them if the staging affected the sale price. Staging should cost a fraction of the value added to the home.

Leave While the House Is Staged

The third rule of staging is: Leave the house while the stagers stage it. Staging is a creative process. It requires no interference from anyone outside the staging crew. Do not worry if you do not like the staging; it is not going to be your house for long. Allow the stagers to turn your house into the home that buyers can imagine as their own and it will pay off.

Leave the Staging Alone

Finally, the fourth rule of staging is: Keep the staging in tact. Do not move or change anything you do not like or that is not *convenient* for you. If your stager takes your television out of your bedroom, so be it. If you absolutely must have a television in your bedroom, talk to your stager about options for hiding it. Remember: the stager's job is to inspire home buyers and to bring out the best in your house so you earn top-dollar. This may or may not include having your television in your bedroom. It's up to the stager. Live with it.

FIXER-UPPERS AND VACANT HOMES

One of the reasons why fixer-uppers take longer to sell, and sell for less, is because they convey exhaustion, work and spending money. Nobody really wants to buy these things and no one wants to come home to it after working all day at the office or on other people's fixer-uppers.

If a home buyer sees only work, work, work to make your house livable, then the views, the size, location *and especially the price*, must give them a heap of inspiration or they will not trade their easy life for the work, frustration and the money required to make your house their dream home.

Make Fixers Livable

If you have a fixer upper, use your top-dollar mindset to make it livable with staging. If you do not make it livable, reduce your list price. Those are your options. Remember: you must cater to the buyer's need to feel your house is easier or more worthwhile than where they live now, as well as their need to feel inspired by the *potential* of the house.

Do Not Pre-Judge the House as a Tear Down

Unless you are selling a literal uninhabitable home that must be torn down, staging earns you more money because staging can make your house seem livable even if it is a fixer-upper. Do not pre-judge a home as a *tear down*. This term is relative. One man's *tear down* is another man's *fixer-upper*.

Buyers who are open to *fixer-uppers* pay more if they perceive that they can live in the house while they slowly fix it up to suit their taste or upgrade. Furniture placement and a few furnishings give them the feeling that the house is not a *tear down* or *fixer-upper*, but a house that just needs some love. If you do not stage a fixer-upper, buyers will not see that the house is homey and livable. They will take one look at the work and head for the hills (or make you a low-ball offer). Staging makes them pause and think about the reality of what actually needs to be done immediately.

Bottom line: If a home buyer can live in the house while fixing it up, staging it will net you more money and better offer terms than not staging the house. Failure to stage a house will always cost you money. To maximize profits for a *fixer-upper*, you must clean, paint, re-carpet and stage it.

Vacant Homes Must Be Staged

Contrary to your instincts, vacant homes do not feel spacious and inspiring; rather, they often feel hollow, empty, cold and they make buyers feel that way. This is especially true for teeny tiny houses and extremely large houses. Empty bedrooms seem smaller without furniture and buyers may think the rooms are too small for their own furniture. When this happens, many will not bother to measure the furniture or the rooms before they move on to a house where they can clearly see that furniture fits in the room. Another common money drain for vacant homes is an ambiguous floor plan. Placing furniture in these areas can erase the ambiguity and make it clear how one can live comfortably in an unusual space.

What Happens If You Choose Not to Stage

If you do not professionally stage your house, be prepared to accept less money for your home than you will receive if you stage it. If you cannot afford to hire a professional stager, you are leaving some money on the table because professional staging adds value that you will not be able to capture on your own if you do not stage. This does not mean you should make no effort at all.

Make Whatever Effort You Can

Again, you may not accomplish everything your top-dollar mindset wants you to accomplish. If you cannot afford to professionally, stage, make sure rooms are used for purposes that are consistent with the obvious purpose for the rooms, remove clutter and create a warm and inviting space.

For example, if your office desk is set up in the kitchen, living room, or dining room, you must move it to one of the bedrooms or the family room. If your dining room table is in one of the bedrooms, move it to the dining room or eat-in kitchen. Although many will applaud your creative use of the rooms, the house needs to *make sense* to buyers who may or may not share your ability to think outside the box.

There are times when it may be too much trouble to stage the house. This is not *top-dollar mindset* but it is all right. Just remember you are leaving some money on the table when you choose to forego staging in a Pottery Barn® world.

GET OUT

When you decide to sell your house, you must realize and accept that your house is no longer your castle or your identity. It is just a house you want to sell for the highest price possible. You have to make space for home buyers to visualize, dream and become inspired by the house in order to earn top-dollar and the dream premium. If you can, you should move out when you list and show your house. If that is not possible, then it is imperative that you live in your house like it is no longer your house.

Live in a Hotel

Imagine your house is now a hotel somewhere between where you used to live and where you are going to live once your house sells. This is part of your top-dollar mindset. You must move on emotionally, intellectually, and in habit, for a new owner to buy the house. Your house should not be cold or impersonal. It must be clean, staged and you should be absent from the house in every way shape and form, and at all times, during the showings so potential buyers can feel inspired to make your house their home and live the life of their dreams.

The Hidden Psychological Barrier

There are actions that drain buyer inspiration, and thereby drain home seller dollars. If a home seller, their family, dogs, cats, snakes, whatever, are in the house while the house is shown to prospective buyers, the buyers are distracted and cannot imagine your house as their home and therefore cannot imagine the house giving them the life they seek. A hidden psychological barrier pops up when sellers are present while buyers are looking at the house. Home buyers can only see the house as inhabited by the seller, the seller's family or the seller's pets. They just cannot see themselves living there.

Every Word You Say Will Cost You Money

Hanging around before, during and after showings talking up the attributes of your house is a barrier to offers and a distraction. Potential home buyers are so distracted they quit thinking about the home and begin thinking how they can leave. They will act polite and listen to you, but they will later tell their agents how they never thought you would quit talking and let them leave. This is the truth and deep down you know it because you said the same thing when it happened to you while you were home shopping. Please understand: this is nothing personal against you. It is just business. It is about selling your house for as much money as possible. These buyers will probably never come back to your house. If you do this to enough buyers and agents, you erode the value of your home because the buyers and agents do not want to see the house for fear that they will have to listen to you try to *sell* them the house.

The moral of this story is: Get Out! Leave before the house is shown and do not come back until the coast is clear. Your presence as a seller is damaging if you are physically present, however, even hints that you are living in the house can trigger these psychological barriers. Remove all evidence anyone lives in the house. This is no joke. Put away clothes, dishes, toiletries, shoes, personal photos, refrigerator magnets, toys, etc.

Be Invisible until Inspections Are Negotiated

Be invisible until the inspections are negotiated. It is only after inspections are negotiated, that the psychological barrier is no longer a threat to the sale of the house, and the house can be sold amicably. It is entirely appropriate to be in the house once the contingencies are removed. It is wise for home sellers and home buyers to meet near the closing of escrow to personally ritualize ownership transfer of the house.

Put Up With Impromptu Visits

One last thing: Agents will sometimes call to preview your house, or to show it to clients, at inopportune times. Many a seller has been caught in the midst of a major cleaning or project, when an agent has shown up unannounced with the buyer for the house. It's Murphy's Law. It is not always convenient. The agents are sometimes rude. The agents do not always follow the directions for showing the house. When this happens, stop and ask yourself: What is my primary goal here? There is only one top-dollar mindset answer: sell the house for top-dollar.

Have your house ready for showings and be as flexible as possible so it may be shown. Put up with inconveniences and last minute showings. Keep the top-dollar mindset and move on.

Okay, now, start packing!

• *Secret Four* •
ELIMINATE OR MINIMIZE
BUYER TURN-OFFS

A lot of things can automatically turn buyers off to a house and cause home sellers to lose money. Suffice to say, it all starts at the curb and goes from there. This area is where having a top-dollar mindset can save you thousands of dollars.

ELIMINATE, MINIMIZE OR LOSE MONEY

Some of the turn-offs can be eliminated or minimized; others cannot. Your top-dollar mindset goal is to eliminate or minimize the impact of all automatic turn-offs. Remember: Each turn-off you eliminate or minimize brings you more money. Each one you ignore, costs you money.

Permanent Defects

Some sellers own homes with turn-offs that cannot be eliminated. Chances are, they purchased their home for less than other comparables homes that did not have the defect, because the turn-off existed when they purchased it. They, in turn, can expect to receive less when they sell the same home, unless they do something to minimize that defect.

If this is your situation, you must minimize it and adjust your price expectations at the beginning. Now, of course, you hate to hear this, but *lower the price*. Get real. Do not fool yourself about automatic turn-offs that cannot be eliminated. Accept this reality. They matter to buyers, even if they do not matter to you, so live with it.

If you price the home as if the turn-off does not exist, you will inevitably price your home too high. In the end, you will lose money because you will end up lowering your asking price below market value in order to get it sold, long after the 30-day buzz is gone, and your house has acquired a costly stigma. Accept the things you can not change. Price it right at the onset to get top-dollar.

Explain Mysterious Defects

Some turn-offs are not obvious but will be addressed sooner or later. Do not put off the inevitable. For example, if you know the home owner's dues for your condominium are way above the average for your area, give a credible explanation up front. Home buyers are spooked by inconsistencies and may or may not take the time to investigate before moving on to another home. Give them explanations for anything that seems mysterious or where your house deviates from mainstream expectations. Make the inconsistency or mystery pay off wherever possible by demonstrating the value in it. Using the same example, the value in the higher dues might be that, unlike other condominiums, the dues include earthquake insurance.

COMMON TURN-OFFS AND WHAT TO DO ABOUT THEM

The following are common costly turn-offs and what you may do to eliminate or minimize them. Each house is unique and your house may have a challenging issue not addressed in this list. Nevertheless, the top-dollar mindset, along with this chapter, will assist you in handling your particular situation.

Road Noise

Home buyers do not like intense road or freeway noise. They also do not like having a busy thoroughfare next to their house. If your house has loud road noise or is next to a busy street, you must lower your price accordingly. All things equal, the adjustment for road noise or proximity to a busy road will be 10-20% below the closest comparable sale that lacked road noise. The degree of noise and proximity to a busy road are subjective and tolerance levels vary from buyer to buyer, so the price adjustment will vary.

Some actions can minimize road noise, such as dual-paned windows, fences, walls and fountains. Do not think for a minute, however, that these eliminate the noise and road issues in the minds of home buyers. Such actions only make it easier for home buyers to accept your house if they are open to road noise and proximity to a busy road. You earn more money if you minimize the impact of the defect than if you do not minimize it at all.

If you are close to a busy road, you must completely fence the property. A home buyer who accepts the noise may have small children or pets and find it easier to accept the house if the property is adequately fenced to prevent their children and pets from wandering into the roadway.

Fences

Except in neighborhoods where it is customary to have no fences, broken down or rotting fences around the property are a turn-off because they represent a big expense that must be made immediately if the buyers have children or pets. If you are selling a rural property, it is even more important since your buyers will likely own horses, dogs or livestock they want to keep fenced. Even buyers who do not have pets will want to keep the neighbor's children and pets, and other people, off the property.

Neighbors

There really is not much you can do if your neighbors have not mowed their lawn since forever, have a Pit Bull in the backyard or their house paint looks like a peeling onion.

The best you can do is to minimize the visibility of these neighbors from the interior of the house. Sometimes, this is critical or you could wait a long time to sell your home.

For example, one man was selling his house. Before the open house, he opened his bathroom windows. Unfortunately, the neighbors' windows were so close that the neighbors could see down into the bathrooms when the windows were open.

Imagine this for a minute. You have entered a bathroom and you can see outside a window and you realize if you can see out – in this particular case – someone *out there* can see *into the bathroom*. How does this idea make you feel? Like running for the hills!

A bathroom is a private space and there should be no possibility that anyone might intrude upon that space, whether real or imagined. Buyers are spooked from houses by their imagination all of the time, so do not give them anything to let their imagination run wild – especially in the bathrooms!

One solution to this problem is to plant fast growing trees or bushes outside the window to ensure privacy. There are, of course, many solutions. In order to get top-dollar you must find the one that works for your house and do it.

Owners, Renters, Children & Pets

Home buyers hate it when the owner, the owner's pets, or children are at the open house or present during the showing. The only top-dollar advice to give is this: Get out and stay out! Do not come back until the coast is absolutely clear. Home buyers are looking for a new life and it does not include you. If you cannot leave, do not say anything except hello unless asked a question about the house.

Home buyers really hate it when you tell them everything you have done to the house in any kind of detail. Remember: *home buyers buy emotionally and justify rationally*. If they are truly interested in your house, they will have their agent ask the questions of your agent.

The best way to communicate the upgrades is a list on the back of the home flyer. The buyers can read the list and revel in your upgrades without feeling like you are trying to *sell* them the house.

Leaking Plumbing

If you have leaking faucets, plumbing or even broken irrigation lines in the yard, fix them. Home buyers are turned off to a house with leaking plumbing. They imagine a late night plumbing disaster and that is the end of their thoughts about buying your house. Remember: we are creating a dream house feeling; not visions of plumbers in dirty clothes in your kitchen in the middle of the night at $200 per hour on Christmas Eve!

Dirty Carpets

A small spot here and there is not a big deal, but big ugly, gnarly stains and smelly carpets are just plain ugly. Buyers want the home seller to replace the carpets. Do it ahead of time to eliminate the problem or find a really good carpet cleaner to make the spots disappear. Leaving the spots and giving a money credit for new carpets is nice, but just seeing the spots turns buyers off and they will think so little of your house they will not even arrive to the point where they learn about a carpet replacement credit. Do yourself a favor and replace them. It is a relatively inexpensive fix that will bring money to your door by providing that inspired feeling that the house is clean and easy to buy from you. Buyers will pay for the convenience of not having to pick out and install the carpets themselves. They pay less if they are buying more work and ugly, dirty carpets. Remember: Buyers pay more for easy and clean.

Dirty Bathrooms

Home buyers turn up their noses at dirty bathrooms. Keep the bathrooms spotless. One vexing detail that makes the bathroom seem dirty is moldy bathtub caulking. Everything can be spic and span, but if the caulking is gross, the whole bathroom looks filthy. Always install new caulk. If you have white tile and a white tub, use white caulk, not beige or gray. You can keep the caulk white by spraying it with a mixture of three-fourths water and one-fourth bleach from a spray bottle every two weeks. Keep all toilets clean and the lids down. If you hate to clean bathrooms, hire someone to do it or just remind yourself that each time you do, you are literally putting money in your bank account.

Food Smells

Home buyers really, REALLY hate smelly houses. It is best if you do not cook in your house while it is on the market. If you cook something spicy, microwave popcorn, or even eggs and bacon, just before a showing (and this inevitably happens, of course), the smell that was so yummy to you will irritate and distract buyers. Odors linger several hours after you have cooked in your house. Some owners will bake cookies or cinnamon rolls during open houses. This is fine, but other foods like toast, eggs and anything spicy just make your house smell SMELLY!

Bedding and Laundry Odors

Another source of smelliness comes from bedding and clothes. You sleep in your bedding about eight hours a day. That is the same as wearing a set of clothing. Oils cling to bedding and do not always come out in one washing because you sleep in them more than one night. Those oils can make your closets, cupboards, drawers, bedroom and bathroom smell offensive to buyers.

Always, place your dirty laundry in a closed hamper. Wash your clothes or have them dry cleaned each time you wear them. Purchase new bedding, including sheets, pillow cases and towels. Wash sheets, pillow cases, blankets and towels every third day and double rinse them each time. Between washings, use candles and lightly fragranced air fresheners to cut down on odors. Avoid strong fragrances such as perfumes.

Pet Odors

Pets are another source of bad smells. Relocate the kitty box or clean it each morning and evening to minimize the odor. Wash all dogs, and their beds, once a week. If you have horses or livestock, muck the stalls and paddocks twice a day and haul manure away weekly.

Cleansers

Do not over-do-it with the bleach and cleansers. Use environmentally friendly cleansers where you are able, and use minimal amounts of other cleansers, to cut down on the antiseptic smell that sometimes inhabits houses. Crack open windows when possible to allow rooms to air out.

Cigarette, Pipe and Cigar Smoke

If the house has a strong smell of cigarette, pipe or cigar smoke, you must paint and re-carpet at a bare minimum to maximize your profits. This may not cure the smell, but it will at least reduce the odor to a low roar and make it seem faint and livable. The objective is to make your house not smell like anything at all. If you do not soften or eliminate smoke smell, you are leaving thousands of dollars on the table.

Clutter

How you feel about your house is a lot like how you feel about how you look when you leave the house for work. If you feel like you look good, good things happen. If you feel like you look bad, bad things happen. Dress your house for success!

Remember the doll collection? Home buyers CANNOT see past the clutter. They take in way too much information in a short amount of time to be distracted by your collections, books, papers, movies, toys, dishes or whatever. Be honest with yourself about clutter. Everyone has clutter and no one likes it. It has to go when you sell your house. If you cannot be honest with yourself or you just cannot face the task, hire an organizer or stager to direct the clutter to storage. You will feel better about your house, and so will home buyers.

Removing the clutter gives you a chance to purge and pack. You are going to do it sooner or later, so why not make money doing it? A de-cluttered house sells for more than a cluttered one every time! Keep reminding yourself you are taking a box of dollars to the bank each time you take a box of your clutter to storage.

Extra Vehicles

This sounds picky, but buyers are turned off to a house even before they go inside when they see cars in the driveway, in the cul-de-sac or on the street near a house. It makes them feel crowded. They also hate to see old cars parked in front of the house. They just drive by and never look inside the home. This goes for RVs, campers, pick-up trucks with horse trailers, motorcycles, farm equipment, bicycles and boats too. Put these items in storage, give them to charity, or sell them so you can park your car in the garage. You will feel a lot better about your house, and so will buyers, when they see a nice clean open driveway with room to park their car in the garage. Again, removing these items will turn into cash in your pocket.

Lack of Storage

Homeowners put their extra clothes in odd places: the garage, extra bedrooms and even the kitchen cabinets! This is because they have far too many clothes to fit in their closets. This is a HUGE buyer turn-off. Even if you have plenty of storage, this makes buyers think there is not enough storage space in the house. Pack non-essential items in boxes and stack them neatly in the garage.

Dead Landscaping

Dead plants makes everyone feel depressed. You do not want that, so water it, change it and hire a gardener. Home-buyers do not stop to think how easy it is to fix this problem; they will drive by your house without a second thought. Remember: No one is sick in this house and everything thrives here, so do not let the yard die. Water regularly and eliminate dead or dying plants from inside and outside the house. Clean bark is nicer than dead leaves. Buyers pay more for clean, easy and healthy.

Bad Curb Appeal

There are entire television shows devoted to curb appeal. First impressions are the most important. All of it must be clean, neat and charming. Buyers literally drive by houses that lack inspiring, clean and neat curb appeal. It is difficult to entice buyers to go inside a house to see the amazing interior remodel if the exterior is uninspiring. Agents hang signs that say "Must See Inside," but that is not always enough to inspire buyers to do so. If your house has charm, but it is obscured by cars, dead landscaping or a bad paint job, fix it. If visitors come to your house and they are not sure where the front door is located, this can be a serious turn-off for home buyers. Make the path to your front door obvious, and inviting, to solve this problem.

Overstating the Truth

Home buyers are completely turned off if you say there is a view of the Golden Gate Bridge, but there is only a view if you have to peer amongst branches of a tree in one corner of one room while standing on your tippy toes. It just is not really true, so do not put it in your advertising. Instead, tell your agent to tell seriously interested buyers about the secret peek-a-boo view of the bridge. The secret view will delight a buyer who is already emotionally drawn to your house while an overstated claim will only turn-off others before they even have the chance to connect with the house.

Boundary Lines

If you are selling a rural property you must carefully and clearly explain all boundaries and easements to your agent and potential buyers. If you have unresolved boundary and easement problems, it is best to hire a real estate attorney to resolve them prior to listing your home for sale so that you can explain the problem and show potential buyers you fixed it. Uncertainty concerning these types of issues is a recipe for a low-ball offer if you are lucky enough to receive an offer under these circumstances.

Always remember: Uncertainty equals less money.

Telephone Poles and Power Lines

If you have a great view but it is marred by a busy telephone pole or a lot of power lines, do your best to mitigate this problem. You might be able to camouflage it with staging. This will not entirely hide it but may make it more palatable. If you cannot mitigate this problem, you will have to accept it and reduce your price expectations.

· *Secret Five* ·
HOME IMPROVEMENTS MUST ADD EMOTIONAL VALUE

People buy emotionally and justify their purchase rationally. This is no cliché. It is truth. The new roof, new windows and foundation upgrades mean nothing to home buyers unless and until they emotionally connect to your house.

Home improvements that add inspiration value, or convenience value, will lead you to get top-dollar for your home. Remodeling and upgrading that does not provide these kinds of emotional value, may be satisfying for you while you live in the home, but is ultimately a money drain. Use your top-dollar mindset to choose upgrades and remodeling that adds emotional value wherever possible.

Some home improvements not only justify their purchase, they also *inspire* home buyers if they create a *feeling* of inspiration such as when a wall is replaced with windows to bring in light or a breathtaking view.

When home buyers emotionally connect, their rational mind wants to agree with their emotions. Home improvements, seen and unseen, are then processed by buyers and their agents to calculate their offer price and evaluate the fairness of your list price. When home buyers look at the home improvements and see they equate to easy, stress-free living, and if your list price matches the value the buyer places on these improvements, then they *cannot wait* to buy your house. And when they cannot wait to buy it, they do not want anyone else to buy it, so they will offer top-dollar.

If you want to improve the value of your house, do it with an eye toward maximizing your return for each dollar you spend. Add inspiration value and emotional convenience value to aim toward top-dollar. Remodel long before you sell your house so you can enjoy your handiwork.

SPEND MONEY TO MAKE MONEY

If your house needs paint, carpet, landscaping or anything for basic livability, such as fixing fences, toilets and heaters; spend the money before you list your house.

Spending this money will eliminate objections from buyers which will otherwise justify a lower price or monetary credit for repairs. Thus, spending this money actually saves you money.

It also creates value and makes you more money because the amount of money you put into paint, carpet, landscaping, etc., is relatively small compared with the exponential emotional value new paint, carpet, landscaping and fixing essentials adds to your house in the hearts of buyers.

AVOID OVER-IMPROVING AND BAD REMODELS

Before you head for a kitchen designer and contractor, speak to a trusted and knowledgeable real estate agent about what buyers are looking for in your neighborhood. Pay close attention to costs for expansion and upgrades.

Some home owners *over-improve* or *badly remodel* their house resulting in a substantial loss when they sell.

Over-Improvements

A house is *over-improved* when the money spent on purchasing the house, plus the amount spent on improvements, is more than the amount a buyer will pay for the home when you sell it.

Steer clear of expensive upgrades so unique in color, style or theme that the vast majority of buyers for your neighborhood will not appreciate and pay for the upgrades. If your neighborhood is full of traditional style houses, and the majority of people in your town are interested in traditional style houses for families with young children, it may be fiscally risky and unwise to rebuild your house into a three story modern structure with industrial style fixtures, counter tops and colors.

Buyers love to buy over-improved homes because they know that they reap the reward of having a remodeled home without having to pay the retail price for the remodel. Since you, as the seller, paid for the over-improvement, steer clear of this situation.

Bad Remodels Can Lower the Value of Your Home

A *bad remodel* means you spent money on upgrades or remodeling, but the appearance or quality is ghastly, or renders the house unusable to the majority of buyers.

Clashing colors, clashing textures, strange alterations to floor plans and random rooms in random places without flow, are common examples of *bad remodels*. The result is an enormous money drain because you not only fail to profit from the remodel, but you do not earn back all of the money you spent on it.

You must also avoid reducing the value of your home with your *remodeling*. For example, if you buy a four bedroom home and your remodel reduces it to a two bedroom home with a family room, you probably reduced the value of your home and you will not be reimbursed for all of the money you spent on the house remodel.

Play to Your Audience

If the majority of home buyers for your neighborhood are families with infants or toddlers you should avoid an expansion and remodel of your house that includes dangerous decks and a split floor plan where young children will be at risk when separated from their parents. The children soon grow up and the parents will want to give them privacy and want privacy of their own, but parents with young children do not see this inevitability. If the home buyers in your neighborhood have small children then they are seeking an open floor plan with the master bedroom and at least two other bedrooms on the same level. Always, make sure your remodeling caters to your audience for resale purposes if you want to maximize your return on the remodel.

The moral of the story is to pay close attention to the costs you pay for upgrades and keep them in line with expectations for the neighborhood. Keeping a top-dollar mindset with regard to remodeling projects means you make conscious choices about how and when to remodel or improve your home.

Make a Plan

Use your top-dollar mindset to take a logical approach to determine which projects will add inspiration value and emotional convenience value to help you choose worthwhile projects instead of wasteful projects.

Start with a fixed budget and make a list of things that will make your house more emotionally appealing. The best way to do this is to look at the inspection reports and listen to advice from your agents and stagers. If they are professionals, they will tell you what gives the best bang for your buck and what are absolute *must dos*. Keep in mind some improvements are a matter of emotional aesthetics, like cosmetic upgrades, while others are about emotional convenience, such as repairs to toilets and the like.

Once you have a budget and a list, circle at least 4 items likely to increase the overall beauty of the house. Examples are new paint, refinishing hardwood floors, new landscaping and a new or freshly painted front door and entryway. Then circle at least 4 items likely to reduce objections from serious buyers. Examples are replace broken windows, broken systems, repair dry rot or treat the house if it has termites.

Once you have circled these projects, analyze the relative costs versus the benefit of the projects and determine which projects will likely give you the most inspiration value and emotional convenience value for your budget. Once you have a short list; start immediately with estimates for each of those items and get to it!

· *Secret Six* ·

EARLY INSPECTIONS & DISCLOSURES MAKE YOU MONEY

EARLY INSPECTIONS & DISCLOSURES PAY OFF

Buyers will inspect the house, so why should you pay for inspections? Because you want to know what is wrong with the house before:

- *you determine the list price;*
- *the house is shown and buyers ask questions; and*
- *the buyer's inspector tells you what is wrong with it.*

Why do you want to know these things? Knowledge is power.

If you have your home inspected BEFORE you list it, you have time to fix the *minor* things that need fixing before buyers seen them. If fewer things are wrong with your house, your house is more emotionally appealing and buyers will have fewer reasons to reject your house or offer less for it. They also pay top-dollar for the convenience of having a home that is in great condition. Although buyers have a certain tolerance level for imperfections, fix things that need fixing to get top-dollar.

Avoid Costly Surprises

If you inspect ahead of time, you have fewer surprises, and so will interested buyers. It is no fun to find out your house needs forty-thousand dollars worth of foundation repairs when you are half-way through escrow. Talk about a deal killer. Find out before you list so that you are not surprised and put at a sudden disadvantage.

High Repairs Can Cost You Nothing if Disclosed Early

Knowing about *major* needed repairs BEFORE you list the house allows you to collect repair estimates and disclose relevant repair estimates to interested buyers before they write their offer.

Put yourself in the buyer's shoes for a moment: High repair estimates are easier to swallow if you know about them before you make an offer, right? Giving inspection reports to buyers before they write an offer makes it easier for the buyers to accept defects before they purchase your home. High repair costs are a moot issue if the buyers plan to remodel, expand or upgrade. If you do not tell them before they write their offer and they find out during inspections, the buyer is more likely to request a price reduction or credit for the repairs. They are also more likely to cancel their purchase.

Do Not Let Your House Develop a Stigma

The more information you have about repairs, the better equipped you are to negotiate a fair agreement about repairs and avoid falling in and out of escrow so many times your house loses its appeal and acquires a stigma. If you home acquires a stigma, buyers lose confidence in the desirability of your house. When this happens, you earn less for it.

For example, let's say there is a huge crack in the foundation and mold is growing on a wall inside the house. If you do not give the buyers a report explaining what is going on and how much it will cost to fix, the buyers will move on to another house that has fewer unanswered and risky questions. The ones who stay interested will

ALWAYS overestimate the repair costs in their mind and write lower offers taking into account their imagined worst fears.

If you negotiate blind, it costs you thousands of dollars. Give buyers the solution up front, or better yet, fix the problem. If you fix it, not only will your bargaining position improve but you will earn more for your house because it will be *easy*. This is top-dollar mindset.

Get the Scoop from Your Inspector First

BUT, you say, the buyers will want to do their own inspections, even after I have already conducted inspections, so why pay the cost of my own inspection? Maybe, you say, their inspectors will not catch everything. Do not bet on it.

No matter what information an inspector who is chosen by the buyer gives you, you will not trust it because you did not select the inspector. You will be guessing without confidence. This will put you at a psychological disadvantage when you negotiate because you will not necessarily have time to do your own inspections and obtain repair estimates from people you know and trust. You do not want to put yourself at a disadvantage with so much money at stake.

AVOID LITIGATION OR LOSING THE DEAL

The disclosure rule is simple: If you have or know information about your house that will affect 1) whether a buyer will want to buy it, or 2) how much they will pay for it, then *you must disclose* the information. It is a simple rule that will keep you out of court or arbitration if you follow it.

Emotional Convenience Value Goes Up If the Seller Is Honest

The thing about disclosure is the buyers will figure out whatever it is you are hiding or omitting anyway, so disclose in advance to heighten the buyer's sense of honesty and fairness about you. Home buyers will pay more for a house, or will forego a price reduction request, if they perceive the home seller is honest and forthright about the home's defects. This is emotional convenience and confidence that increases the value of your home.

There are, of course, certain things that will not be obvious to home buyers and therefore they must rely upon your honesty to disclose them. Examples are whether the property has ever flooded, claims made against insurance policies for fire, stains on the floors or counter tops that are covered by rugs or appliances, and failure to obtain permits for improvements. Disclose them. You don't want the buyers to find out when they talk to your neighbors.

Avoid Losing the Deal When the Defect Is Discovered

Home sellers are fearful of disclosing these and other things about their house because they think they will not earn as much money for the house if they disclose it. The fear is well founded. But, this is precisely the reason why they must disclose the things they know will affect the value of their house to buyers. Remember: Defects can be entirely acceptable to buyers because of the reasons already mentioned or because the buyers plan to remodel or upgrade and the disclosure becomes a non-issue and costs them nothing. Failure to disclose the items, however, may be discovered during escrow and cause the deal to fall apart or, if escrow closes, may become a lawsuit upon later discovery. It is easier for the home buyer to accept the defect if they know about it and know the home seller has been living with it without consequence.

If You Disagree With Your Agent

If you and your agent have a difference of opinion about disclosing certain information about a property, have your agent consult their legal department for a final decision. They always advise disclosure. As an alternative, you may obtain a written legal opinion from your attorney telling you whether it is necessary to disclose the information.

• *Secret Seven* •
SELL AT THE RIGHT TIME

THE BEST TIMES TO SELL

Home sellers often speculate about when is the best time to sell their house to maximize profits. Before you consider timing strategies for your sale, you should review the difference between a seller's market and a buyer's market.

What is a Seller's Market?

A Seller's Market is when there are very few homes on the market and a lot of buyers looking for homes to buy in that market. The sellers will see more than one buyer want to purchase their home because there are just not enough homes for sale to go around. Sellers who sell in a buyer's market often see more than one buyer attempt to purchase the home, i.e., multiple offers for the home. Prices tend to rise in a seller's market because buyers will pay more for homes when they are in short supply.

What is a Buyer's Market?

A Buyer's Market is when there are a lot of homes on the market but not very many people looking to buy homes. The sellers will wait longer for buyers to look at the house and write an offer. It can take months to sell your home in a buyer's market because buyers have a lot of homes to choose from and they are looking for the seller who is the most motivated and will give them the lowest price. Prices for homes tend to come down as sellers seek to find a willing buyer for their home and must compete with many, many other sellers to do so.

The Optimum Time to Sell is a Seller's Market

When timing your sale there is one rule that always holds true: If you want the highest price possible, regardless of other circumstances in your life, sell in a seller's market, and do not ever sell in a buyer's market.

Of course, the reality is you move when you need or want to move or when it makes financial sense to do so. Sometimes this means you must sell in a buyer's market. There are advantageous times to sell your home even in a buyer's market.

Sell When the Need Arises

If you want to move because you need a larger house, smaller house, different house in a different neighborhood, changed jobs, are getting married, having a baby, getting divorced, or must sell for any other reason, then the best time to sell is when these needs arise regardless of market conditions.

The Entire Family Must Be Ready To Move

It is imperative that each family member be absolutely committed to selling your house and moving before you put it on the market; otherwise you are wasting your time and money, and only setting yourself and the rest of the family up for disappointment and conflict.

For example, one family failed to sell their home after their daughter resisted the move to the point where she refused to put the lock box out for agents when they called to show the home and sabotaged showings and inspections by breaking windows and writing expletives on walls.

Another example is a family who lost a family member. All of the family members wanted to sell the house except for one who did not want to move because she could not bear to part with the house and the memories she had of the family member they had lost. She made it difficult for the family to clean and stage the house and to make needed repairs. The family members were in dire conflict until they finally realized they had to wait until she processed her grief before the house could be sold for top-dollar. Although the family could have sold the house for an as-is price, they earned more with her cooperation.

These examples are extreme, but they illustrate the best time to sell your house is when each family member is committed to moving. Only then, can you have a successful and profitable experience selling your home.

THE BEST SEASONS

The best times to show and sell houses are in the spring, summer and autumn. Houses look better, the weather is more cooperative and statistically there are a lot more escrows and sales at these times. People just feel good, are more optimistic about the future and look at houses during these seasons.

There is a biological drive in the spring to build a nest and, another, in the autumn, to find a nest for the winter. Peak activity occurs during those seasons. Do not be surprised if activity is slow in July and August due to vacations and the start of the school year.

If You Choose to Sell During Winter

If you must sell in winter, make it as easy as possible to show and sell your house. Be prepared for lack-luster activity and buyer reticence to make a solid offer. Buyers are less motivated and more cautious about their future prospects during January and February. They are reluctant to move in the rain, snow and cold, so they buy when the weather is warm and dry. Still, take heart: There are always those who relocate in winter and must buy a house. Some houses, of course, are located in winter sports areas. For those homes, winter is also a good season to sell.

MAX OUT TAX-FREE CAPITAL GAIN

The federal long-term capital gain tax policy permits home sellers to keep a large tax-free portion of their capital gain from the sale of their house. When does the government give big tax breaks? Not very often, so take advantage of this tax law. Tax laws change with regime changes, economic conditions and federal and state budget needs, so this law may not last forever.

How it Works For a Single Homeowner

Here's how it works: If you are single and have lived in your house for 2 of the last 5 years, you may sell your house and pay no capital gains tax on up to $250,000 of your profit. According to the long term capital gain tax rate of 15% (which may change like any other law), you keep $250,000 tax-free, but pay a 15% capital gains tax on any capital gains made above $250,000.

Here's the math:

- *Price You Paid For Your House* *$500,000*
- *Price You Receive For Your House:* *$1,000,000*
- *Tax-Free Capital Gains You Keep* *$250,000*
- *Remaining Capital Gain* *$250,000*
- *Tax on Remaining Capital Gain.* *$37,500*

In this example, you pay $37,500 to the U.S. Treasury for the sale of your house. Home owners remain in their houses because of the convenience; however, they are paying 15% of every dollar they earn in equity after the initial $250,000. Is it worth it? Maybe. Maybe not. The smart money says sell and start the tax-free capital gain money clock again.

If you time the sale of your house, you may avoid paying the tax. Here's how: Using the same example, watch for when your capital gain for the sale of your house reaches $250,000. Then: sell it. Take the tax-free $250,000 and run with it. Buy another property with all or part of it and start the tax-free capital gain money clock all over again in an area that has a similar rate of appreciation as your old house.

How it Works for Married Homeowners

Married home sellers keep up to $500,000 tax-free.

Here's the math:

- *Price You Paid For Your House* *$500,000*
- *Price You Receive For Your House* *$1,000,000*
- *Tax-Free Capital Gain You Keep.* *$500,000*
- *Remaining Capital Gain* *$0*

- *Tax on Remaining Capital Gain. $0*

Married home sellers pay no capital gain tax because the long-term tax-free capital gain maximum is $500,000. However, this married couple will pay 15% for each dollar of capital gain they earn above the $500,000 tax-free limit. Thus, if their house sells for $1,250,000 instead of $1,000,000, they will pay 15% of $250,000, or $37,500, for capital gains taxes.

These are simplistic examples, so you are advised to consult your tax advisor, certified public accountant and your estate planning attorney, concerning your situation before you use this strategy.

SELLING STRATEGIES FOR CHANGING MARKETS

Markets have a life of their own. They go up. They go down. The market for your home changes for two reasons: 1) the number of homes on the market which are competing with your home for a buyer goes up or down, or 2) the number of buyers shopping for homes like yours, goes up or down.

Many things affect the number of homes that come on the market and the number of buyers looking for homes. The news, whether it is correct or not correct, affects decision making about selling or buying a home. An increase in jobs, or increase in unemployment, affects the number of homes on the market for sale and the number of buyers looking for a home. Interest rates can cause buyers to decide to look for a home or can cause them to refrain.

Suffice to say, there are a lot of forces in the world that affect the decisions of home buyers and home sellers. The bottom line is that the number of buyers and sellers make the market a seller's market or a buyer's market and that, in turn, affects the value of homes.

Since it is impossible to predict the future, use the following basic market guidelines when selling your home, but be flexible if the conditions of the market suddenly change, are uncertain or volatile.

Sell Late in a Seller's Market

If you are selling in a seller's market where prices are rising, you should put your house on the market at the latest possible moment so that you can maximize your sales price. Beware this strategy carries some risk if the market suddenly changes direction.

Avoid Riding the Market Down if a Seller's Market Changes

If you are selling in a seller's market that turns into a declining market before your house is sold and there is little hope the market will turn positive during your time horizon for selling your home, you should sell as soon as possible to avoid riding the market down.

For example, a home seller relocating to another state had already purchased her new house. When she put her old house on the market, she listed a little bit above market value because the market was rapidly rising. Unfortunately, the market changed direction and prices started to decline. She followed the market down by matching her price reductions to other sales as they went down in value over a nine month period until she realized the market was not going to turn around any time soon. She did not want to rent the house so she reduced her price slightly below her competition to attract a buyer. Her house sold immediately and she moved on to her new life. Had she listed her house at market value when she originally listed the house, she would have earned thousands more than she ultimately earned for it.

There is always the risk the market will change direction at the moment you reduce ahead of the downward trend, but it is impossible to predict when that will happen. Pay close attention to market changes in a volatile or uncertain market.

Selling in a Sharply Declining Market

If you are selling in a buyer's market and prices are in sharp decline, with no end in sight, think carefully about staying in your home until the market improves. Consider renting your house and buying a new one in the buyer's market to improve your real estate wealth portfolio.

If you nonetheless wish to sell, four things are necessary for you to sell your home for the highest possible price under such extreme conditions:

1) *you must be highly motivated to move to the point where there is no other option;*

2) *your house must show better than other homes listed within ten percent of your list price;*

3) *you must price the house lower than other homes that show as well as your home; and*

4) *you must have and act upon a top-dollar mindset.*

WHERE WILL YOU GO WHEN IT SELLS?

If you sell your home, where will you go? You have two options. You can move out *before* you sell your home or *after* you sell your home.

Move Out if You Can Afford it

If you can afford to buy your new home, or move into your rental, before listing your home for sale, then do it. It is the most advantageous for negotiations and the most convenient for all concerned. Be very careful that this strategy does not backfire. For example, one couple bought their new house before they sold their old house. Although they could afford to make two mortgage payments while they waited for their old house to sell, the financial stress was hard to bear. Sometimes this kind of stress can cause sellers to take low-ball offers to eliminate the stress. This is not the top-dollar mindset. Make sure you are financially and emotionally prepared if you choose this option.

If You Must Stay, Make it Contingent

If you cannot afford to buy your new home until you sell your old home, make the sale of your home contingent upon finding your replacement home and require an adequate rent back period after you close the sale of your home so you may close escrow for your new home and move into your new home.

Do Not Wait to Search for Your Replacement Home

Sellers who fail to search for a replacement home until their home is under contract for sale are headed for trouble. You may think there is no need to look for a new house until you sell your house, but there are good reasons to look before you list your home for sale.

First, if you have not yet listed your home, looking at homes will educate you about prices, market conditions and help you decide whether it makes sense to give up the life you live in your home or not. You do not want seller's remorse, so make sure you have an idea what you can afford, and what to expect, once your home is sold.

Second, you will narrow down the area and other attributes you need and want for your new home.

Third, once your home is sold, you usually have about two weeks to find your replacement home and secure it under contract. You must have a handle on pricing, availability and have a few homes already in mind; otherwise, you sign up for additional stress. Moving is already one of the most stressful events of your life; do not add more stress by delaying the inevitable. Go look at houses and pick out a few in case your house sells right away. It *will,* if you have a top-dollar mindset.

BUILD WEALTH: DO NOT SELL

The best long-term strategy for building real estate wealth is to turn your old house into a rental and earn rental income. Homeowners who employ this strategy are *wealth builders* because they have a long term view about building a portfolio of properties that will eventually yield rental income in the form of rents as well as future appreciation. If you are able to employ this strategy, do so.

If you change your mind after renting it for up to three years after you moved out, you can still sell it and keep your tax-free capital gains under the current tax laws. If you wait past the third year, you can always move back into your home for two years, sell it, and max out your tax-free capital gain.

• *Secret Eight* •

PRICE IT RIGHT TO MAXIMIZE PROFITS

SUPPLY AND DEMAND

We discussed supply and demand, and how it affects your timing when you are selling in a seller's market or a buyer's market in the last chapter, so we will not give a long explanation here.

Just remember:

- *a Seller's Market is when there are very few homes on the market and a lot of buyers looking for homes to buy in that market, and*

- *a Buyer's Market is when there are a lot of homes on the market, but not very many people looking to buy homes.*

Just because you sell your home fast, doesn't mean you sold it for top-dollar. When the supply of homes for sale is low and the number of buyers looking to buy a home is high, your home can sell quickly, but might be priced too low.

FOUR PRICE OPTIONS

As a home seller, you have four pricing options:

- **OPTION #1:** List your house at a price BELOW MARKET and likely receive multiple offers for more than your asking price. This strategy ensures that you earn the highest possible price in the shortest amount of time. You will have a lot of interest in the house, a lot of showings and a lot of attendees at your open house. You should have offers within a week or two.

- **OPTION #2:** List your house at a REALISTIC PRICE OR FAIR MARKET VALUE and likely receive an offer within a month or two. You will have steady showing appointments and solid open house attendance from buyers until your home is sold.

- **OPTION #3:** List your house at a PRICE SLIGHTLY ABOVE FAIR MARKET VALUE (but in the ballpark) and likely receive an offer within ninety days or more. You will enjoy regular showings, good open house attendance and positive feedback. If you do not provide adequate inspiration and emotional convenience value, you may expect an offer below your asking price.

- **OPTION #4:** List your house at a PRICE WAY ABOVE FAIR MARKET VALUE (ten percent or more) and watch would-be home buyers move on to a better priced house. You will see no offers after ninety days and little activity after the initial 30-day buzz, except for neighbors who are wondering if you are really going to earn your price or not because they are thinking about selling their house.

AGENTS DO NOT *GET* YOU A PRICE

One of the most common misconceptions about real agents is the belief that agents somehow *get* you a certain price for your home.

Sellers who operate with this belief will interview agents and hire the one who recommends the highest list price. This is a big, big mistake.

Avoid Desperate Agents

Some agents are desperate for a sale, or another listing to add to their quota. They will tell you a high list price just to get you to agree to hire them to sell the house. They sincerely hope you get your price, but deep down they know it probably will not happen and they will ask you for a large price reduction within a month or so.

Do not make the mistake of automatically hiring the agent who recommends the highest list price. Use your top-dollar mindset and your own common sense after speaking with at least three agents to determine the list price that will attract buyers *and* maximize your profits.

Now that you understand supply and demand, you know that buyers set the price because they have the money and the price they offer has more to do with what they can afford, whether or not they are inspired and whether they expect competition when they offer to buy your house.

Hire an Agent With a Top-Dollar Mindset

Professional agents who have a top-dollar mindset will tell you what they *think* a buyer will pay for your home, based on supply and demand, their understanding of what buyers are looking for in the market, and the sales price of similar homes recently sold in your neighborhood. Yes, agents make a guess. It is an educated guess, but it is still a guess. It is not a promise because market conditions change moment to moment.

Agents with a top-dollar mindset make you money by telling you what needs to be done to close the gap between the as-is price and the top-dollar price given the market conditions.

When you decide to sell your home, you and your agent will review recent sales, also known as *comparable sales* or *comps* to aid you in deciding upon a list price for your home. Before you hire an agent, make sure they regularly work with home buyers (not just sellers) and ask them what average buyers in the market expect for the price you are asking for the house.

The Market Does Not Care What Price You Want

Another mistake sellers make is they tell their agent they want to list their home for the price they *want* to receive for the home regardless of market conditions or the comparable sales. The market does not care what price they want. Buyers determine the price they will pay. A seller must decide if they are willing to accept that price. Of course, there is always room for negotiation, and sometimes, sellers get the price they want. But, make no mistake: Neither the seller nor the agent determines the *sale* price. The buyer *and* the seller determine the sale price.

Your job, as a seller with a top-dollar mindset, is to make buyers want to pay the highest price possible for your home.

THE 30-DAY BUZZ

The first thirty days your house is listed for sale are crucial for earning top-dollar. The majority of motivated home buyers, and their agents, will see your house within the first thirty days your house is on the market. If the list price for your house does not ring true, the agents and would-be buyers will move on to another house and completely forget about your house.

Homes Show Better If Priced Fair

What is a fair price? A fair price takes into account all of the attributes buyers are using to determine the price they will pay for the life they will live in your house. Home buyers are not stupid. They are obsessive compulsive about looking at houses and they do not miss a beat. They scrutinize each house for all of the points of value and they mentally add and subtract based on what they see. If you give them inspiration and emotional convenience value, buyers will add numbers to their offer price.

A better priced house does not necessarily mean a lower priced house. Buyers are looking for value for the price. Not just the price. How a home *shows* is every bit about the price. If the price does not match the value provided, intangible and tangible, then it does not *show* well and is passed up by buyers and agents.

Pricing High and Reducing Later

You may choose OPTION #4 and think you can always lower your asking price if you receive no offers. Big, BIG MISTAKE. Why? Because nobody cares anymore. Houses are like buses; there is always another one coming. The buyers, and agents who are working with buyers, who thought your house was overpriced are sure to find another house next week if not sooner. They are not waiting around to see if, and when, you reduce your price – they MOVE ON to a better priced house. Meanwhile, your house acquires a *reputation* for being over priced with unreasonable sellers.

Once a buyer has moved on, they never reconsider your house – unless you drastically reduce the price. In that case, you are far from top-dollar.

DAMAGE CONTROL

Real estate agents are the most enthusiastic about, and show buyers, the houses that offer the best value. That is what they are paid to do and, frankly, the best agents do it well.

If you chose OPTION #4, and listed your house too high the first month your house was on the market, the chances are good that agents for potential buyers saw your house and only remember some vague notion your house did not *show well* so they do not show it to their clients.

So what do you do if you made a mistake and listed your house too high in the beginning and it's been three months with no meaningful offers?

The BEST OPTION is to take it off the market for a couple of months and bring it back on the market at the new lower price. There is no need to change agents to do this. In fact, it is completely unfair to list your house at an unrealistic price, contract your agent to advertise and spend hours showing your house in vain, only to switch to another agent when you finally decide to be realistic about your asking price. There is absolutely no benefit to you by changing agents; unless, of course, your agent is a louse. Even if you hold open houses, and re-advertise at the new price, you will see but a fraction of the traffic you saw the first week your house was originally on the market.

The SECOND OPTION is to lower the asking price by *A LOT.* What is a lot? A lot is enough to move you *into the ballpark*. So, if your house is listed 20% too high, you need to reduce by more than 20%. If your house is 10% too high, then you reduce by more than 10% to move into the ball game. You might get the market's attention. Or not. But, you might sell your house.

The THIRD OPTION is to lower the price just a little bit

without reaching the ballpark. This option, when taken, causes all of the torture related to house selling and ends in the house seller desperately lowering the price months and months, or even a year later, with a third or fourth agent, at a higher commission rate, and accepting a price lower than they would have achieved had they priced the house *in the ballpark* at the beginning. Home sellers with a top-dollar mindset do not choose this option.

THERE IS ONLY ONE REASON A HOUSE DOES NOT SELL

What should you do if your house has been on the market for several months with no meaningful offers? You may be tempted think you have no offers because your real estate agent did not hold the house open or advertise enough, you should have painted the middle bathroom, it is wintertime and the flowers are not blooming, or because there is a busy street running in front of your house, BUT NONE OF THESE THINGS MATTER. The only reason a house does not sell is the price is too high. If the price does not match what is offered, the house will not sell. The worst part is that if this is happening to you, you are bound to lose thousands of dollars.

Time and again, home sellers who over price their home end up reducing, reducing and reducing their list price to a point where they must reduce their house to a value far below what they could have earned had they priced the house at market value at the beginning of the 30-day buzz when the majority of buyers were interested in the house.

Sellers with a top-dollar mindset do not make this mistake. Sure, they may push the envelope a little and price it a little above market value, but they also provide enough inspiration and emotional convenience to make the house worth it.

· Secret Nine ·
Use Effective Advertising

ADVERTISING IN AN INTERNET WORLD

Ok, here's the truth about real estate advertising. Are you ready? The advertising that works and gives you the most bang for your buck and your time are the following:

- *internet*
- *photos*
- *multiple listing service*
- *real estate agents*
- *open houses*

That's pretty much it. Nowadays, if you list your house with an agent, your house will be listed on the Multiple Listing Service (MLS) for your home's area and beyond. The MLS is literally a list of all the homes listed for sale with agents in your area. All agents for your neighborhood have access to all MLS listings.

Great Photos Are Essential

It is absolutely imperative that you give buyers GREAT PHOTOS when your house is listed on the MLS. This is another reason why you ***must stage*** the house!

Here's how it works and why: When you list your house with an agent, the agent will list your house on the MLS and add photos to the MLS listing. The MLS listing is then vectored to other real estate home search websites where the public may look for homes. Buyers who are, or are not yet, represented by an agent peruse home listings at real estate home search websites such as:

- *Realtor.com*®

- *Re.Cleanoffer.com*

- *Greathomes.org*®

- *other local real estate company websites*

HOW BUYERS SEARCH FOR HOMES

Buyers log on to a home search website that is directly linked to the MLS. They check boxes on a computer page to designate the community, number of bedrooms and baths, square footage and price range they desire. They press *enter* and all of the MLS listings fitting their criteria pop up on the computer screen.

Buyers shop the listings looking at the *photos* of each home. They look at your home photos to determine if the house feels like home, makes them want to trade their existing life for the one in your house, makes them want to go to your open house, or makes them want to call a real estate agent to see the house. They judge whether they want to see your house *solely* on the photos.

If the photos are bad, buyers will not bother to see the house unless their agent talks them into seeing it. Some agents do not bother to see homes that lack inviting photos because they anticipate that the house will show poorly and will be harder to sell. You do the math.

It is absolutely critical for you to post inspiring photos if you want to earn top-dollar for your house. Just as some buyers will not go to see a house with lousy photos, some buyers just *know* when they see *their* house on the internet based on seeing the photos alone. Photos bring more buyers to your home and more buyers mean there is more competition to buy your home. More competition to buy your home means you get more offers and get top-dollar for your home.

NEWSPAPER ADVERTISING

What about advertisements in the newspaper? The only newspaper advertising that consistently produces qualified buyers directly to houses for sale is the Open Home Directory. The Open Home Directory section of the local newspapers show which houses are open for buyers to see (usually, but not always, on Saturdays and Sundays). This works because a buyer may see your house on the internet and then look in the directory to see if your house is open for them to see on the weekend. Of course, home buyers may see if the house is open from the internet advertisement, so the continuing efficacy of newspaper Open Home Directories is definitely waning. Still, there are some, albeit, very few, who still read the Open Home Directory, so, depending on your area, it might be worth advertising your open house in them.

THE TRUTH ABOUT OPEN HOUSES

Few people fall out of the sky and find their new house during an open house. Although a buyer for a particular house may appear out of nowhere and instantly buy a house that is held open, this is an extremely rare event. The majority of serious home buyers are working with an agent and their agent shows them houses.

So, are open houses a waste of time? Absolutely not, but it pays to be realistic about what they may and may not do for you. Having a top-dollar mindset means you want to expose your home to the market as much as possible, but do not want to make wasted efforts.

Who Goes to Open Houses?

You may expect that about fifty percent of the attendees will be neighbors and lookie-lus who just saw the signs and decided to stop.

The remaining attendees are actual home buyers in various stages of readiness to buy a home. Some are just starting and do not have any idea what they can afford, while others have made a career out of looking for a new home.

This should not discourage your from holding open houses. There are some profitable reasons to do so.

Why Hold Open Houses?

If a home buyer is very serious and motivated to buy a house today, their agent will show them houses – often on a weeknight after work or weekends.

The strongest reason for holding open houses is to allow serious buyers, who saw your house with their agent, to see your house *again* in a more casual setting without their agent. This helps buyers take their time looking at your house before they make an offer. It gives them time to feel more connected to your house. This is a great benefit to you because you will have fewer fly-by-night offers from buyers who haven't spent enough time in the house to make a solid decision. An open house allows serious buyers another opportunity to see your house to add up the emotional convenience and inspiration value.

Another reason is sometimes even serious buyers may not schedule a private showing with their agent owing to scheduling conflicts.

Finally, if a home buyer working with an agent is not quite ready to buy, their agent may *send* the buyer to view houses during the weekend open house. This is more convenient for buyers who are waiting for their house to sell or otherwise not quite ready to make an offer if they find the right house. Of course, if you have done a good job providing emotional value and inspiration, you never know, they just might like it enough to *get motivated*, even if they are not quite ready.

Agents Who Do Not Believe In Open Houses

Some agents do not believe in open houses and do not hold them at all. Some agents are lazy and others are part-timers or listing machines with other priorities. Still other agents reason that a buyer's agent will show the house if the buyer is really serious, so they may not hold it open. Although there is some merit to this argument, for the reasons previously stated, houses should be held open as often as is reasonable under the circumstances.

Forget Open Houses On Holidays

It is always a good idea to hold a house open the first four weekends the house is on market. It makes little sense to hold an open house on a holiday. If a serious buyer is using the holiday to see homes, they can make appointments to do so.

Hold it Open When Other Houses in the Neighborhood Are Open

It is a good idea to hold your house open when neighboring houses are held open. You will benefit from the increased buyer traffic. Although, admittedly rare, occasionally a buyer will pop into an open house while they are on their way to see a neighbor's property. Occasionally they buy the house they did not plan to see!

Make Signs Visible and Plenty

Finally, make it easy for buyers to find the house and they will truly appreciate it! Make sure your agent has placed the signs in logical traffic pattern turning points and the signs are clearly visible for car drivers. This is especially true when the roads are narrow and winding. A test run is advised.

LONG-SHOT ADVERTISING

Other than the Open Home Directory, real estate advertisements in the newspaper, or in those fancy glossy real estate magazines, do little to advertise your house and really only advertise the agent, real estate company or permit you to *show off* your list price for your home. This advertising may indirectly benefit you because a buyer may call the agent and actually make an appointment to see your house. More often, the buyer calls about your house, but purchases another house. Glossy magazines often advertise homes that are already sold by the time they are seen.

Even if a newspaper or magazine advertisement shows a photo of your house, the advertisement is essentially for the benefit of your agent, or your ego, and the advertisement is *highly unlikely* to sell your house. It is not uncommon for agents to receive no calls at all from these advertisements and it is not because the advertisement is bad. It's because that is not really how serious buyers shop for a home in the internet age.

So, why do agents do this? They want to assure home sellers they are doing everything they can to sell the house and because this is how agents obtain more clients. They may not be able to sell your house to the person who calls, but perhaps they may sell another house to that caller. This does not mean your agent is only advertising your house in the paper to advertise for new clients. It also does not mean you will never attract a buyer for your house this way. Agents are truly trying to attract a buyer for your house. The truth, however, is the odds are very much against that happening from a newspaper or magazine advertisement. Nine times out of ten, the advertisement is a waste of money for your agent and only frustrates you because you see no results for your agent's effort.

Relax. It was a long-shot anyway. The world has changed. The internet has largely replaced newspapers and magazines.

• *Secret Ten* •
MAKE MONEY BY NEGOTIATING

AN OPEN ATTITUDE WILL MAKE YOU MONEY

Negotiation is the single greatest fear of all home buyers, home sellers and most real estate agents. People dread negotiation because they believe negotiation means one person *loses* and the other person *wins*. They also dread it because they take what is said *personally* and *feel* hurt or insulted. In reality, nothing is further from the truth.

If you have a top-dollar mindset, you must follow the first rule of negotiation: The starting point for successful negotiation is attitude.

Do not take anything said, or how it is said, as a *personal attack* on you. Cultivate a detached, optimistic and inquisitive attitude and you will win at negotiation. If you go into negotiation thinking you are going to lose money, guess what? You will lose money. Think positive and be open.

THE DEAL MUST *FEEL* FAIR

The second rule of negotiation is: There will only be a *deal* if those concerned are happy with the deal and think it is a *fair deal*. This is true in no matter what kind of market you are operating. If one party suspects the deal is not *fair*, they will not consummate the deal. If someone *feels* the deal isn't fair, there is no deal. Period. Make it *feel fair* to all concerned and it will work; otherwise, you will only meet with opposition over and over again until someone figures out how to make it feel fair or the parties walk away from negotiations.

Now, you may think in order to *win*, at negotiation, the deal must be a *little unfair* to someone, but that is wrong thinking.

Do not make the mistake of substituting your idea of *fair* for theirs. Believe it or not, some home buyers are less concerned about dollars than they are about buying your particular house or moving in at a time right for them. Some are more concerned with their interest rate than the purchase price. Some are more concerned they get to buy a house on your street because their friends live around the corner. All of these things matter to the buyer and they pay you for them. Your idea of what is *fair* may dramatically differ from that of the buyer and yet, they may not conflict at all.

Harboring an open attitude in negotiations, with an eye toward making the deal feel fair to everyone, including you, will yield more dollars than attempting to strong arm the buyers into meeting your demands. Terms change throughout a transaction so always ask for something in return for something given, to ensure the feeling of fairness on all sides.

YOUR BASIC BARGAINING POSITION

The Third Rule of Negotiation is you must understand your basic bargaining position. Here are the three basic scenarios:

• **SCENARIO 1:** If a home buyer is more motivated to purchase your house than you are to sell it; you, as the home seller, are at a relative advantage in the process of negotiation. In this scenario, a home seller is more likely to earn their asking price or more. This is the basic bargaining position seen in a seller's market or when you get the dream premium.

• **SCENARIO 2:** If a buyer is less motivated to buy your house than you are to sell it; the buyer has a relative advantage in the process of negotiation. This is the basic bargaining position seen in a buyer's market. Sellers are less likely to earn their asking price if they do not provide inspiration and act from a top-dollar mindset.

• **SCENARIO 3:** If the seller is not very motivated to sell the house and the buyers are not very motivated to buy the house, then it is extremely difficult, if not impossible, to reach an agreement for that house to be sold to that buyer. This is a classic no-win situation.

LOSING STRATEGIES

SCENARIO 1 and SCENARIO 3 do not cause home sellers problems because in SCENARIO 1 sellers receive their asking price and in SCENARIO 3 there simply is no deal.

The SCENARIO 2 causes all of the home seller anguish. Here's why: Sellers know they have inferior bargaining position, but do not want the buyer to know it for fear the buyers will take advantage of them. They think negotiation is about winning and losing and they think they are likely to *lose* so they employ a strategy to avoid *losing*.

Ironically, these strategies cause them to feel like losers. This is because they are trying to ignore or hide their inferior bargaining position from the home buyer. Home buyers are not fooled. They know if your bargaining position is weak.

Here's how sellers mess it up: They either make a big stand about something and walk away from the buyer or they give the buyer whatever the buyer asks to avoid *losing*. Either way, the house seller feels like a loser.

If they make a stand and the buyer walks away, they later resent having been so firm. In the extreme, sellers who make a big stand may lose the best offer they will ever receive for their house. This is especially true if the seller is selling in a declining market and they are not conscious of the fact that prices are in decline and they face lower offers in the future.

If the seller gives the buyer whatever they ask for, the seller feels like they gave away the store needlessly and may second guess their decision – or worse – beat themselves up about it for not having stood up for themselves. Of course, this thinking is all wrong.

WINNING STRATEGIES

You are on the road to winning when you realize negotiation is not a process whereby one party *loses* and another party *wins*. Negotiation is a process whereby all parties come to an *agreement*. How can this be? What kind of trick is this? There is no trick. If you want to stay in the win-lose mindset, go ahead – make yourself miserable and lost. If you want to negotiate productively with a top-dollar mindset and positive results for yourself, read on.

Do Not Try to Hide Inferior Bargaining Position

Top-dollar home sellers who have inferior bargaining position *know* they do not have superior bargaining position. Rather than focusing on it and attempting to hide it with losing strategies, they instead seek to increase their bargaining power or work around their inferior position, in a productive way, so that they maximize their profits under the circumstances.

If the buyers have a vastly superior bargaining position, take your home off the market. If you still want to sell your house, forget posturing, make the best of the situation and focus on maximizing your profits by working the process of negotiation and using your top-dollar mindset.

Solidify Areas of Agreement

The PROCESS of negotiation boils down to sharing information and looking for areas of agreement. If there are areas of agreement, those are wins for all concerned.

Transform Areas of Disagreement

If there are areas of disagreement, look for ways to transform them into agreement. This is where the attitude part comes into play.

A lot of home sellers are so focused on price (their number one concern) they forget buyers may be less concerned about price than they are about other aspects of the negotiations. When you encounter areas of disagreement, transcend them by looking beyond your own desires and concerns.

Example: Transform Disagreement about Price Reduction

For example, assume you and a buyer for your home are stuck in your negotiations because you want $525,000 for the house and the buyer wants to pay you only $500,000. You might be willing to take the $25,000 hit, but there could be another way to keep some of that money and sell your house by negotiating the problem.

A *top-dollar mindset* approach to this problem is to ask the buyers *why* they want the price reduction. Assume, hypothetically, that the buyers tell you they want the reduction of $25,000 to $500,000 to accommodate a lower monthly payment so they may qualify for the loan.

If you like the other terms of the offer, like the buyers and do not have another buyer chomping at the bit to buy your house, why not consider paying two *points* to reduce the buyer's payments so they may qualify to buy your house? Here's how it works: Two points equals two percent of the purchase price or $10,500. Two points in today's loan market buys the buyer's interest rate down by about one-half a point, for example from 5.5% to 5%.

Here's the math: The buyer's monthly payment for a conventional loan for a $525,000 purchase price at a 5.5% interest rate is about **$2,980** per month.

The payment for the same loan with a $500,000 purchase price at 5.5% is about **$2,839** per month. The seller must give up $25,000 to reach this payment reduction for the hypothetical buyer to qualify for the loan.

But if the seller pays two points, which is $10,500, instead of $25,000, the buyer's interest rate goes down to 5%. The monthly payment for the $525,000 purchase price is only **$2,818** per month.

The end result is the seller gave up only $10,500 instead of $25,000 and the buyer got the loan.

This is just one example to show how asking for more information, and keeping an open mind about negotiation as a tool to transform areas of disagreement, may result in a win-win situation for all concerned, but especially for you as the house seller – even in a buyer's market.

AGREE TO DISAGREE

But what if you still disagree? If you still disagree, then you agree to disagree and move on. That is agreement too. Where's the *win* in that you say? You win because you attempted to transform disagreement into agreement and you discovered you cannot and now you do not have to waste your time and resources trying to agree or wondering if there is a possibility for agreement.

NEGOTIATE TRANSACTION COSTS

Now that you understand how to negotiate, turn your attention to common transaction costs and expenses you may consider negotiating when working toward agreement and transforming areas of disagreement.

In each real estate transaction, there are certain expenses that will be incurred by the buyer, seller or both. The expenses are largely involuntary. They must be paid by someone in order to close the deal.

These expenses are all negotable. Agents will tell you that the *norm* in your area is the buyer pays for certain expenses and the seller pays for the rest. Despite any supposed *norms*, all expenses are negotiable, so pay attention to these expenses, and who pays for what, and you may potentially save yourself thousands of dollars.

Below are common negotiable expenses:

- *termite, house, fireplace inspection fees*
- *city resale inspection fees*
- *county resale inspection fees*
- *natural hazard disclosure report fees*

- *homeowner's association documents fees*
- *homeowner's association transfer fees*
- *documentary transfer taxes charged by your city*
- *documentary transfer taxes charged by your county*
- *repair costs for termite damage and dry rot*
- *repair costs for broken systems and appliances*
- *title insurance policy expenses*
- *escrow officer expenses*
- *home warranty costs*
- *homeowner's association fees*

Now, you may be thinking: this seems very small potatoes. But they do add up.

For example, in California, many counties charge a documentary transfer tax which must be paid at the close of escrow for the sale of any home within each of those counties.

Marin County charges $1.10 for every $1,000 of purchase price. Assuming a house sells for $500,000, the transfer tax for the sale of the house is $550.00. That tax must be paid by someone at the close of escrow and is negotiable.

Some cities also charge a transfer tax which must be paid at the close of escrow for the sale of any home within the city limits. This tax must be paid in addition to any county tax.

The documentary transfer tax for the City of San Rafael, California is $2.00 per $1,000 of purchase price. It is $7.00 per $1,000 of purchase price for the City of Richmond, California.

Example: City and County Transfer Tax

Based on a $500,000 sales price, the city transfer tax for San Rafael is $1,000. If you add the Marin County Transfer tax of $550 to the City of San Rafael transfer tax of $1,000, your total documentary transfer tax for the home sale in San Rafael, is $1,550. For the City of Richmond, which is located in Contra Costa County, the city transfer tax for a $500,000 home will cost $3,500. If you add the $550 transfer tax, the total transfer tax is $4,050.

Keep Track of Who Pays for What

When responding to an offer, keep track of who pays these expenses and shift the burden for paying these expenses to the buyer as you negotiate terms, or use these expenses as bargaining chips, when transforming areas of disagreement into areas of agreement. One word of caution: do not get too caught up in saving every nickel and dime and lose sight of the big picture.

• *Secret Eleven* •

HIRE AN AGENT WHO WILL MAKE YOU MONEY

YOU MUST INTERVIEW AGENTS

The majority of home sellers will hire a real estate agent to assist them with the process of selling their house. You want to hire an agent who has a top-dollar mindset and who will give you advice that makes you money. He or she must be professional, energetic, organized and must sell real estate in your area on a full-time basis. You hire your agent to sell your house and help you earn the highest price possible, so make sure they will do their job for you.

Agents Are Not Your New Best Friend

Agents are NOT your new best friend, so do not make the mistake of hiring an agent to keep you company. Hire them to help you get top-dollar for your home. That is their job. Interview them with this in mind. Yes, it is good if you like your agent, but they are working for you; not throwing your next birthday party. Take it seriously and hire a professional who will get the job done for you. Always use caution when hiring an agent who is already a friend (or family member) as you may find your experience puts a strain on both your professional and personal relationship.

Get a Referral to an Agent or Meet Them at an Open House

The fastest and most reliable way to find a good agent is to ask your friends, family and professionals for referrals to agents with whom they have had profitable experiences. Ask them if their agents made them money by giving good advice.

Another reliable way to find a good agent is to meet agents in person at open houses. While you are looking at the house, interview the agent. Find out if they have a top-dollar mindset, are knowledgeable, trustworthy and experienced enough to be a candidate for the job of selling your house with you. Later, check their references and testimonials.

Interview Questions for Agents

Before you interview agents, prepare a list of questions for each of them. The list should include information such as:

- *Which comparable sales do you think are important for pricing my house?*

- *Have you seen the comparable sales? How fast did they sell? How many offers did they receive before they sold?*

- *Which houses are my primary competition when you list my house and what can we do to make my house rise above the competition?*

- *How long will it take to sell my house?*

- *What is the profile of the typical buyer for my house and where do they live?*

- *What are buyer's expectations about pricing and terms in the market?*

- *Is financing easy or difficult to obtain for buyers in the market for houses like mine?*

- *How many years experience selling houses do you have? What other professional experience do you have?*

- *Do you have adequate time and resources to service my house listing?*

- *Do you have a schedule for the preparation of the home and a system for keeping track of the mound of paperwork associated with the sale?*

You get the picture. Pay attention to details such as whether the agent is on time, keeps promises and is organized. Among other things, make sure they hold open houses and broker tours, keep fresh flyers in the sign box, update the photos of your home on the MLS and internet sites and advertise your home in the Open Home Directory. Ask them about their system for follow up with agents who show the property and how they will obtain feedback for you to help you change anything that may stand between you and earning top-dollar for your home.

Speaking of top-dollar, ask the agent about their ideas for getting top-dollar. Remember, you are trying to find out if they have a *top-dollar mindset* so ask a lot of questions about how their services may put more dollars into your pocket.

Sometimes agents are hired just because they are fun to be around, or have a pretty face, but upon closer inspection, they are afraid of negotiation or have no clue how to help you bridge the gap between the *as-is price* for your home and *top-dollar.* You want to know this before you commit to them, so ask questions until you know they can earn their keep.

PART-TIME AGENTS

Generally speaking, you probably do not want to trust the sale of your house to a *part-time* agent because they will only have part-time skills and information and your situation will take a back seat to whatever their main gig happens to be, whether it is having a full-time job, running a separate business or having substantial committee and other obligations that prevent them from working full-time. There are rare exceptions. Home sellers are wise to ask questions about an agent's status as part-time or full-time and their other time commitments, to avoid misunderstandings in the long run.

LISTING MACHINES

Besides part-time agents, there are also agents who are essentially *listing machines*. They list your house in the Multiple Listing Service, put up a sign, maybe print a few flyers, and take calls from agents and buyers for your house.

These agents do not generally show the property. They may or may not have an assistant who will show the property. They have so many listings they could not possibly hold all of them open on any given Sunday.

If your house doesn't sell right away, they start, and keep, asking you for price reductions until you capitulate. These agents know if they can induce you to reduce your price low enough, the house will sell, with little or no additional effort on their part.

These agents are fine if you do not want much personal service or attention and do not really want to hold your house open. They are also fine if you do not want to do any of the things necessary to earn top-dollar for your house as outlined in this book.

These are not bad agents; they are just not service oriented agents. You generally pay the same commission price for these agents for no service as you do for agents who give full service. When you hire these kinds of agents, you may leave thousands of dollars on the table.

DISCOUNT AGENTS

Some agents and brokers offer discounts or charge for services on an á la carte basis. Discounts make sense when you are selling in a seller's market because your agent need not spend as much money and time marketing and selling your house as they will in a buyer's market.

In a buyer's market, you need all of the help you can get, so make sure you are very clear with the discount agent about what they will do for you to sell your home in such a market.

Make sure you will receive the same services as offered by other agents who charge a higher commission rate. Sometimes the higher priced commission agents offer additional services that will not really affect the bottom line, i.e., redundant advertising or extravagant entertainment for your first open house for brokers. There is some sizzle to this, but not much steak.

Compare the details about what the discount agent versus the higher priced agent will actually do to earn you top-dollar before you decide to go with either agent. Analyze whether you think the additional commission is worth it or not.

ATTORNEYS

You may decide to hire a real estate attorney to handle your paperwork and negotiations. This works best if you have identified a buyer and do not wish to market your home to sell it for top-dollar. Yes, it can save you commission dollars, if you hire a real estate attorney who understands residential sales and lending practices; however, do not expect them to list and market your home. Let them handle the paperwork and help you negotiate but make sure their tactics do not interfere with selling the house. Hire a lawyer who has assisted many other sellers so that you do not pay for their learning curve.

• *Secret Twelve* •

FOR SALE BY OWNER: SAVE THE COMMISSION, LOSE TOP-DOLLAR

Many home sellers want to sell their houses themselves to save the commission they would otherwise pay agents to market their homes and advise them about the transactions. This is called *For Sale By Owner* or *FSBO*.

There is nothing wrong with this strategy and it sometimes works out; however, for each person who successfully sells their house themselves, there are countless others who try, are frustrated and end up calling a real estate agent to finish the job.

Why is this true?

THE EMOTIONAL ROLLER COASTER

The first reason is home sellers find they cannot handle the emotional roller coaster that comes with marketing and selling their house. Do not take this personally, but greed and fear are the two basic emotions people contend with during the process of selling their house and neither emotion is comfortable. These two emotions may be downright overwhelming and may cause you to make decisions or agreements that do not get you top-dollar because you want the feeling of fear to go away or because your greed distracts you from issues that may come back to bite you in the end.

Many who start off as FSBOs find these emotions – especially the fear - overwhelming and quickly realize they would prefer to be shielded from the emotional roller coaster. They are better able to gain perspective and keep their emotions in check if they hire a real estate agent or experienced real estate attorney to assist them.

COMPLICATIONS

The second reason is selling real estate is a lot more complicated and a lot more work than home sellers think it is. They do not have the time, patience, knowledge and experience to deal with all of the various issues and angles that arise.

Why does it look so easy if it is so hard?

Because successful professional real estate agents spend hours and hours, week after week, studying the market, the inventory, staging, negotiating, networking, sharing information about schools, communities and the marketplace and studying sales and economics statistics, but YOU only see the end result. Plus, agents are not emotionally involved – or at least they should not be if they are professionals. They also shield home sellers from much of the stress and frustration of the negotiations, the trials and tribulations of the bureaucracy of the transaction, the mound of paperwork, scheduling drama and negotiating repairs.

LIABILITY

This leads to a third reason why people who want to sell their home themselves eventually decide to hire an agent. If they go it alone, they have no one to blame, or to point the finger at, but themselves if they are later sued for failure to disclose, fraud or for making legal mistakes.

Home sellers often do not have complete information about their legal obligations and fail to provide legally required disclosures or fail to disclose defects. FSBOs that are lucky enough to receive an offer may flub the deal because they lack sufficient knowledge, negotiating or problem solving skills, or are just plain overwhelmed by the situation. This can lead to a lawsuit. Anyone who has ever been sued will tell you: It's a nightmare! Once they discover that there are legal or disclosure issues, many times, a would-be FSBO seller will hire an agent or attorney to finish the job; Or in some cases, they lose the deal and start all over with an agent.

WHY YOU DO NOT SAVE THE COMMISSION

The third reason that sellers choose to call an agent after attempting to sell their house is they find out they do not really save the commission.

Assume you are selling your house as a FSBO and your asking price is $500,000. Your neighbors hired agents for a 6% commission and sold their houses for $500,000. Their homes are identical to yours, so you figure you do not need an agent, can save the 6% commission and get the same price.

The 6% commission paid in your area is $30,000 for a $500,000 purchase price. This is shared equally between the seller's agent and the buyer's agent, so each agent receives $15,000 for their work and representation for the sale. Here's the math:

- *Purchase Price. $500,000*
- *Minus Commissions at 6%. . . . . -$30,000*
- *Seller Earns $470,000*

Example: Neither Buyer nor Seller Have Agents

Now assume a buyer approaches you to purchase the house and they think the house is priced fairly in relationship to the comparable sales.

If the buyers are not represented by an agent, and you, as the seller, are not represented by an agent, you will think "Yippee – I do not have to pay an agent $30,000! Wahoo! I'm saving $30,000!"

Newsflash!

Home buyers approaching a FSBO *also* think they will save the commission. That is one of the reasons a FSBO is so appealing to them! They think they can buy your house below market value because you are not paying a commission. The buyer is also thinking "Yippee – I don't have to pay as much because the seller doesn't have to pay an agent $30,000!"

A savvy buyer will subtract the 6% commission from their offer price. All things equal, the buyer will logically pay only $470,000 for your house. Here's the math:

- *Purchase Price* *$470,000*
- *Minus Commissions at 0%* . . . . *-$0*
- *Seller Earns* *$470,000*

Did you earn $500,000 for your house? No, you received 6% less for your house. You received only $470,000. Did you save the 6% commission? Yes, but you received 6% less for your house. Did you handle all of the marketing, costs of advertising and headaches? Yep! How is it you benefitted from being a FSBO? Good Question!

You saved 6%. You lost 6%. You spent time and money selling your house without the guidance and professional advice from an agent. In reality, you lost money and time. What's more, you might have sold your house for more if you received advice and referrals from a real estate agent about how to market, stage, photograph and advertise your house to earn top-dollar. You might have sold your house for more than your neighbors received for their homes!

Example: You Do Not Have an Agent, But the Buyer Does

Here's another possibility: A savvy buyer who is represented by a savvy agent asks if you are *cooperating* with agents. *Cooperating* means a seller will pay a commission to the buyer's agent –½ of the usual total commission, or 3%. In this instance, the buyer will pay no more than $485,000 for the house and expect you to pay their agent a 3% commission. Here's the math:

- *Purchase Price. $485,000*
- *Commissions paid at 3% . . . . -$15,000*
- *Seller Earns $470,000*

Did you receive $500,000 for your house? No, you received 3% less. Did you pay a commission to sell your house? Yes, you paid 3% to the buyer's agent. Did you spend time and money advertising and marketing your house and handling the transaction? You betcha!

Is it really worth it? Many find out it is not worth it and that is why even if they try to be a FSBO, they run screaming to a real estate agent to finish the job, get them more money for the house and bail them out of their misery!

But wait a minute! Commissions are negotiable. You say: "I do not have to pay 6 or 5 or even 3 percent to the buyer's agent if I do not want to do so." That's true, but you want to sell your house, don't you?

The point is any intelligent buyer will want to save the commissions too so they do not pay more for the house than it is worth. If the comparables included 6% commissions paid, but your sale includes no commissions, why should the buyer not get the benefit?

CIRCUMSTANCES WHEN YOU *CAN* SAVE THE COMMISSION

The only viable option, if your situation is like the example above, and assuming you can attract a buyer without the help of an agent, is to split the commission savings.

You can also save *part of* the commission by hiring an attorney to handle the paperwork for your sale in special circumstances.

These options are ideal if you already have a buyer for your home and agree upon the terms; such as when you sell your rental property to your renters or when a neighbor tells you they want to buy your house if you ever decide to sell it.

In these cases, of course, you are probably leaving money on the table because you are not exposing your home to the marketplace and not following the advice of an agent with a top-dollar mindset. That's okay. If you are willing to settle for the price offered by your renter or neighbor, your least expensive option is to hire a discount broker or real estate attorney to handle the paperwork. You may save some or all of the commission you would otherwise pay if you quit your day job to sell your house. Just be aware that you are probably not getting top dollar for your home.

If you hire an attorney, hire one who has experience handling residential real estate transactions. Some attorneys understand real estate law and contract, but are not in tune with the marketplace or with the requirements of lenders. If they are not in tune with these aspects of residential transactions, attorneys can kill your deal by lawyering it to death or give misguided advice that ends up costing you just as much as an agent.

The Top-Dollar Mindset Checklist

☐ Hire an agent who has the top-dollar mindset and will make you money.

☐ Memorize and use the mindset question. Will this action:
  1) make me money;
  2) save me money; or
  3) waste my money?

☐ Make home improvements that add emotional convenience value and inspiration value to your home.

☐ Clean the house like the President is coming to visit.

☐ Hire a talented stager to make your home feel inspiring.

☐ Move out, pack up and stay away during showings.

☐ Eliminate or minimize buyer turn-offs.

☐ Conduct early inspections and fix what you can fix.

☐ Pick the best time to sell for you and your home.

☐ Price it to attract buyers and reach for the Dream Premium.

☐ Post inspiring photographs of your home on the MLS.

☐ Negotiate with a positive and open attitude; make sure the deal feels fair; and do what it takes to improve your bargaining position.

www.ingramcontent.com/pod-product-compliance
Lightning Source LLC
Chambersburg PA
CBHW031949190326
41519CB00007B/722